Just Like Me

THE BEGINNING OF CIVILIZATION

Copyright © 1997 Just Like Me, Inc.

Text by
Yaba Baker

Illustrations by
Anne Marie Oldham

Just Like Me, Inc.
Washington, DC 20017
(202) 526-1725

Fifth Edition - Fifth Printing
September 2010

$\pi = 3.16$

$\sqrt{x}^2 = x$

$a^2 + b^2 = c^2$

SIN
COS
TAN
$\div \times + -$

African scientists were the first to create mathematics like addition, subtraction, multiplication, division, and fractions. African scientists went on to create higher level mathematics like geometry and trigonometry. These early discoveries made it possible to later create things like computers, microwaves, and televisions that we use today.

Afican Scientist created the divisions of time (seconds, minutes, hours, and days).

minutes, hours, and days).

Each weekday has 12 hours of the day and 12 hours of the night, which was discovered by African scientists. The scientists discovered that it takes exactly 24 hours for earth to have day and night.

6:00 A.M.

6:00

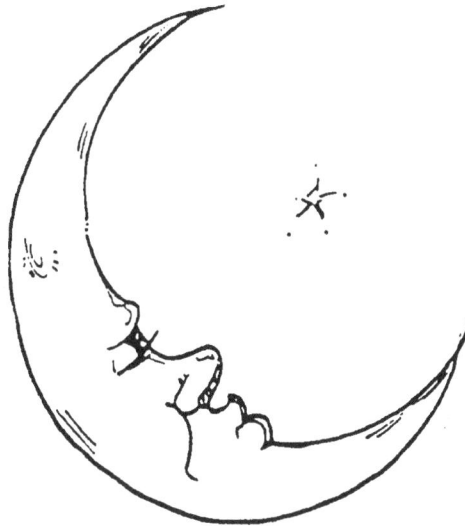

Each weekday has 24 hours in it. When the 24 hours is up, the weekday changes. Monday has 24 hours and when Monday's 24 hours are up, Tuesday's 24 hours begins.

P.M.

6:00 A.M.

African people were the first to create a school of higher learning, which is now called a college or a university.

African people were the first people to farm and use animals to help with farming.

Africans in several different areas of Africa were the first people to invent tools such as hand axes, arrows, and fish hooks which were necessary to build communities.

African people were the first people to build a community into a city with craft workers, soldiers, and priests. The farmers in the surrounding countryside provided food for the city workers by raising wheat, barley, cattle, and goats.

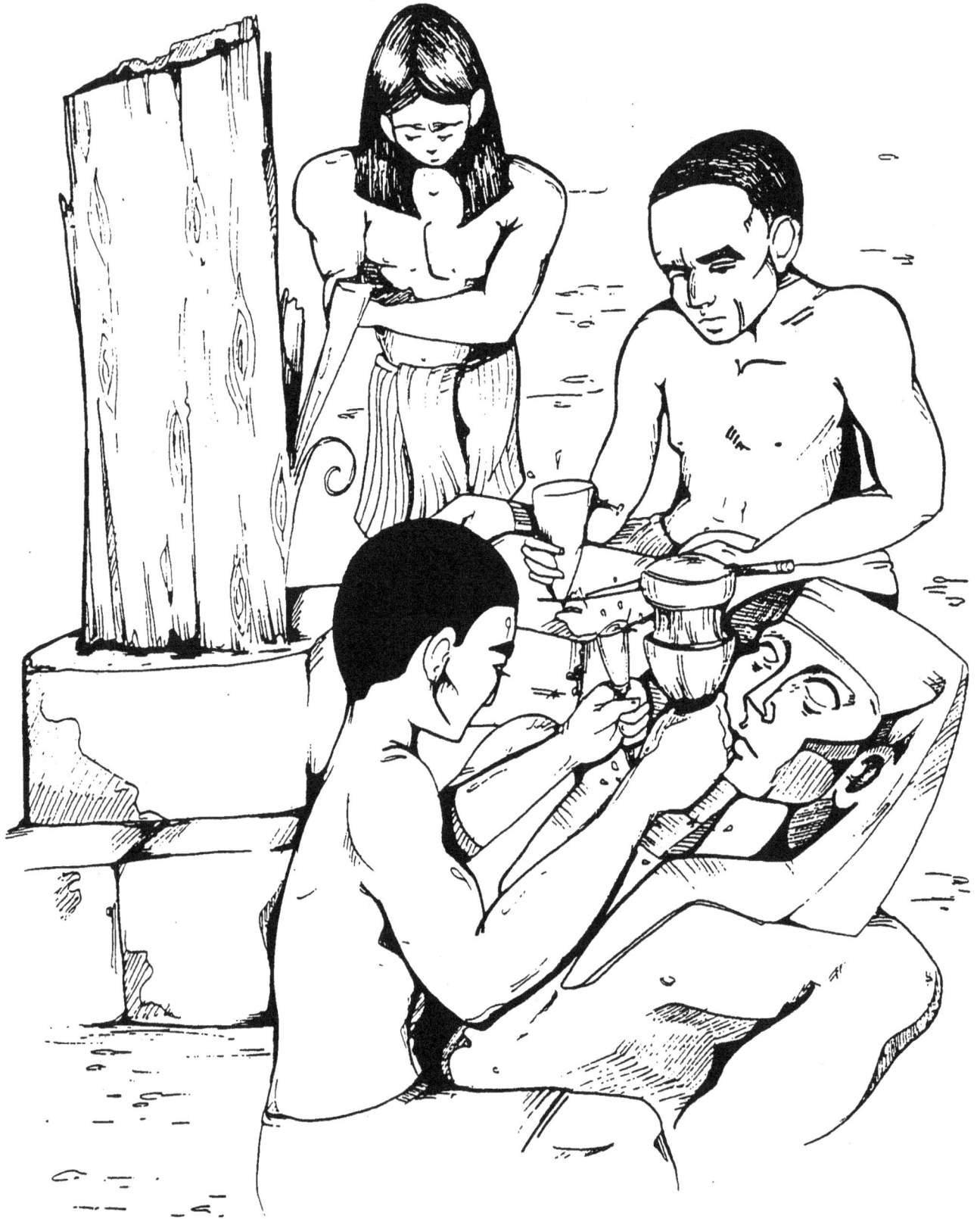

Africans were excellent in creating different forms of art. Statues were made of many different materials from wood to the hardest stone called black diorite.

The first people on earth were Africans.

North America

South America

All men and women came from Africa. As time went on, men and women moved to different parts of the world. The differences in temperature in these various parts of the world caused changes in the features of the nose,

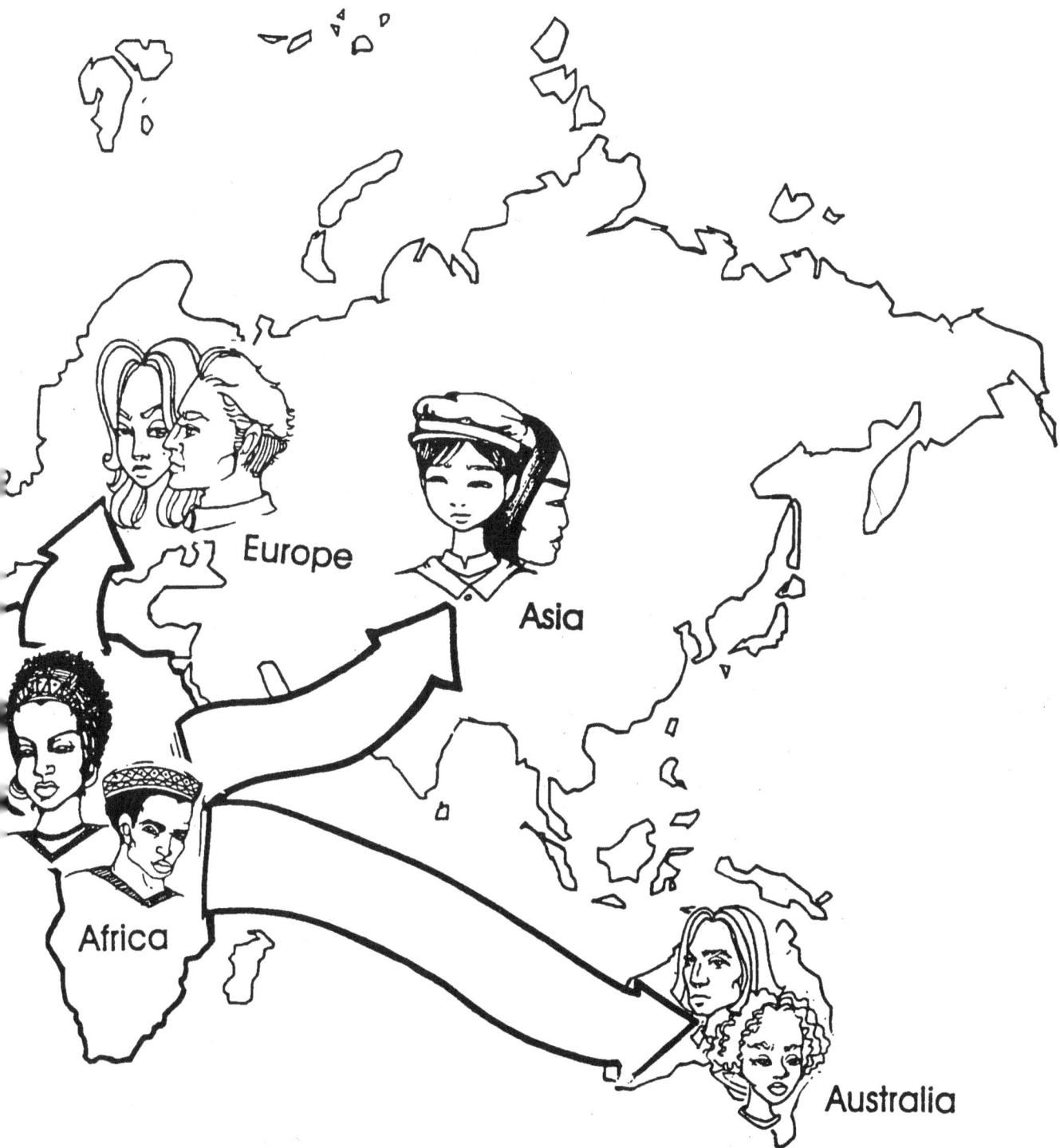

hair, skin color and eye color to adapt to the temperature. This is why there are different races such as Africans, Caucasians, Asians, Native Americans, Latinos and so on.

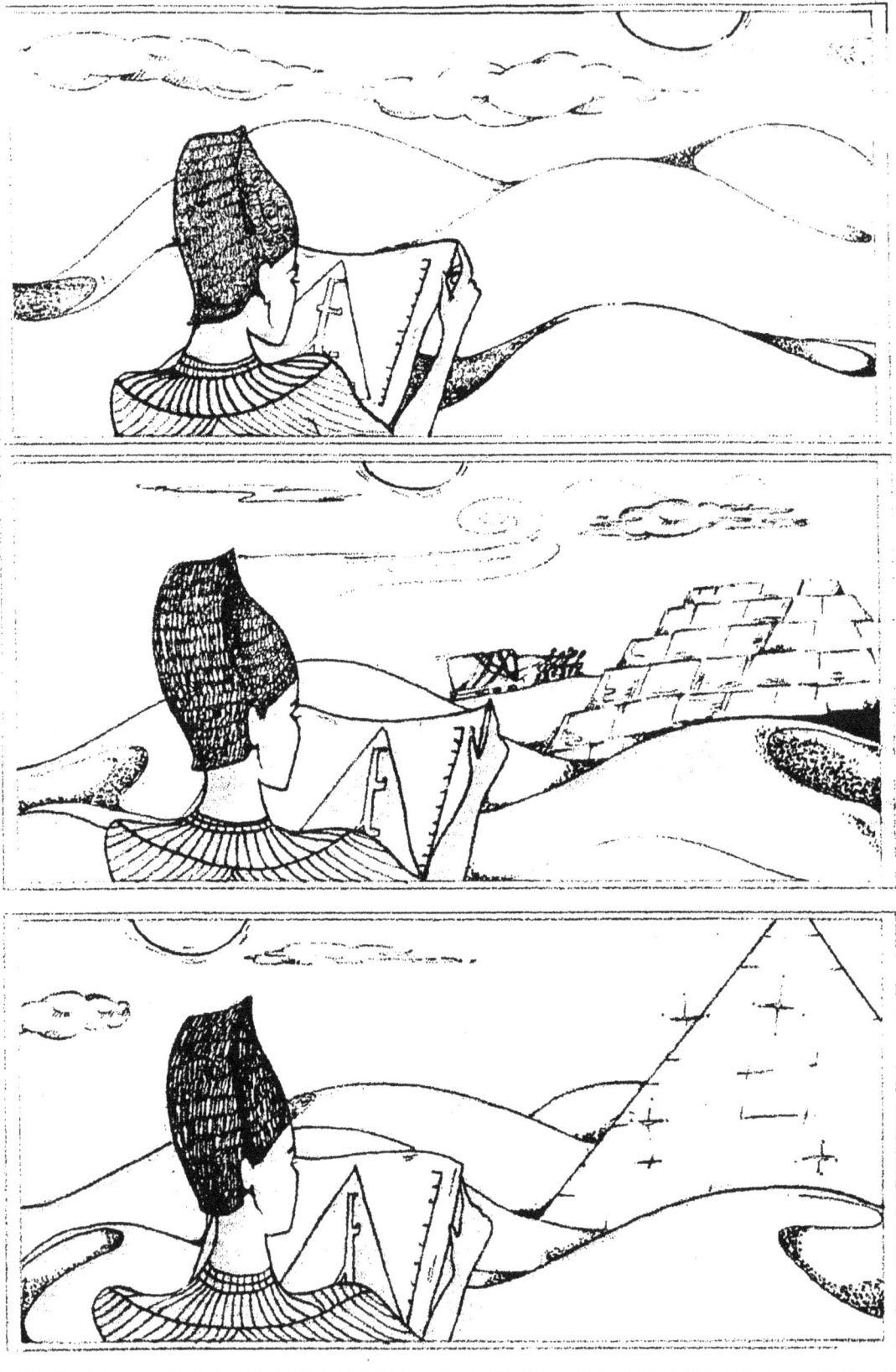

An African scientist and architect named Imhotep built the first pyramid as a place to study the stars, as well as a place to bury dead pharaohs (kings). This pyramid is the oldest standing stone monument in the world, still standing some 4,600 years later.

African architects built the pyramids so precisely, the four corners face exactly to the north pole, south pole, east, and west.

Egypt

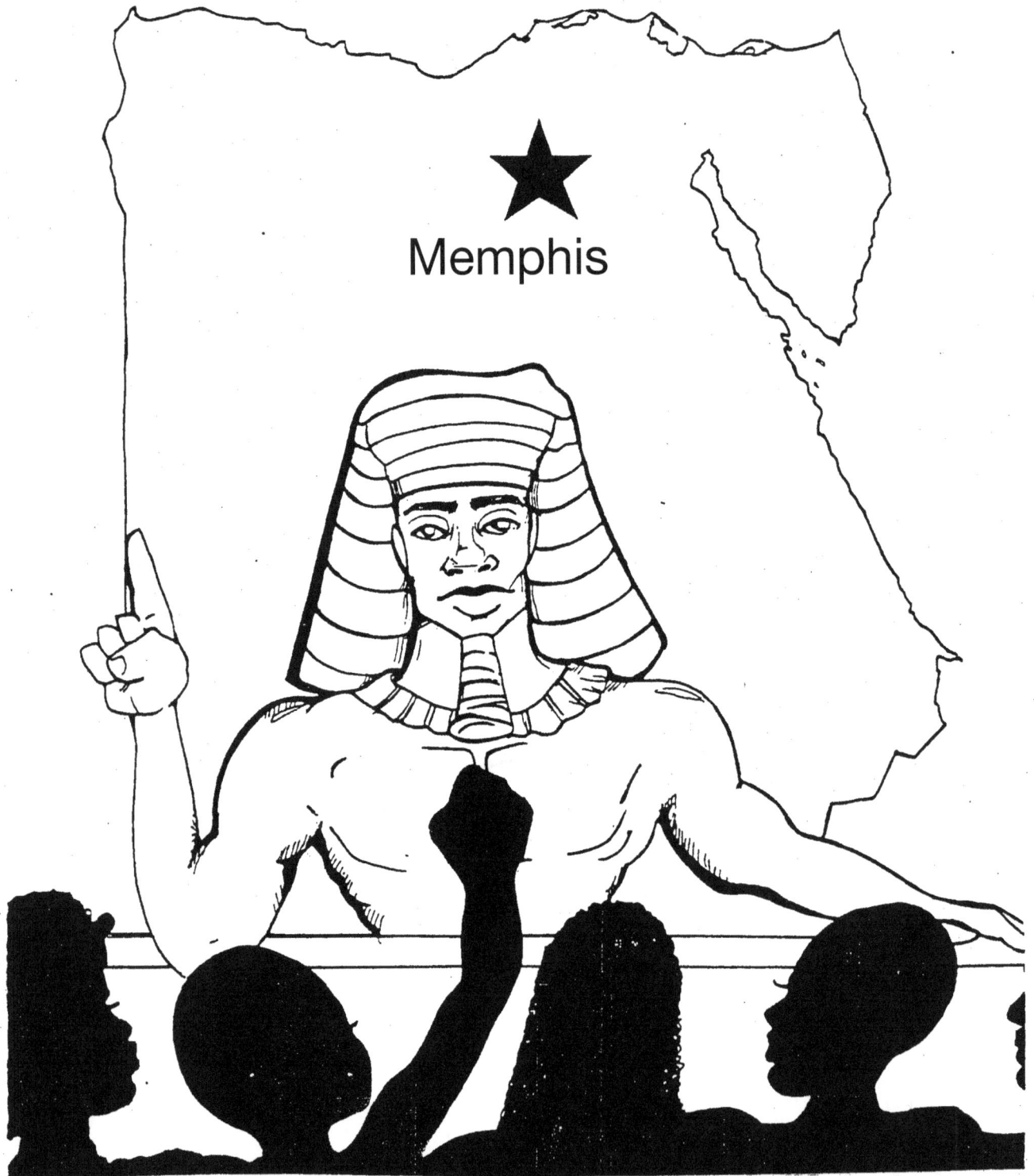

African people formed two territories, which were called the lands of Upper Egypt and Lower Egypt. Later, Upper and Lower Egypt became the world's first unified country. Menes was the king who unified Egypt and created the first known government in the world. Egypt was ruled by a Pharaoh (king).

The Roman Empire
202 B.C.-476 A.D.

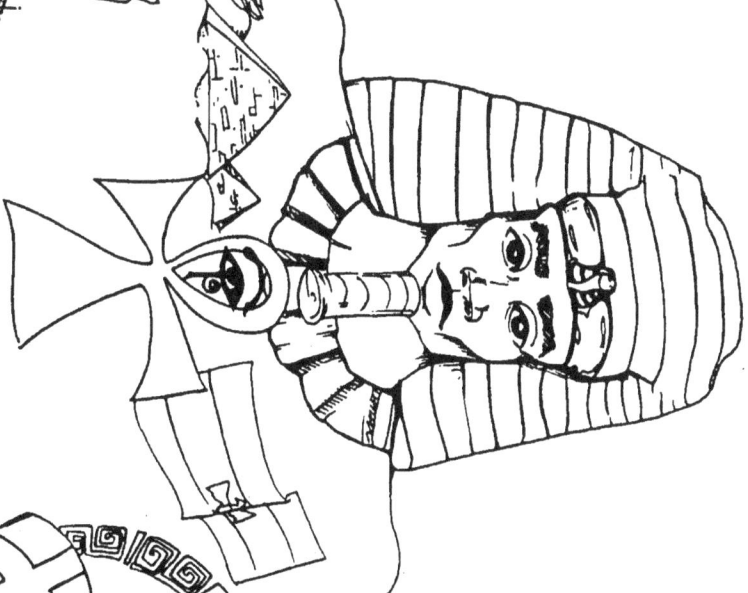

The Egyptian Empire
4200 B.C.-341 B.C.

The Greek Empire
1100 B.C.-323 B.C.

The Egyptian civilization lasted over 3000 years. Roman and Greek empires combined, only lasted about 1400 years. The United States is only 234 years old. Therefore, the African civilization is one of the oldest known civilizations in the world.

15

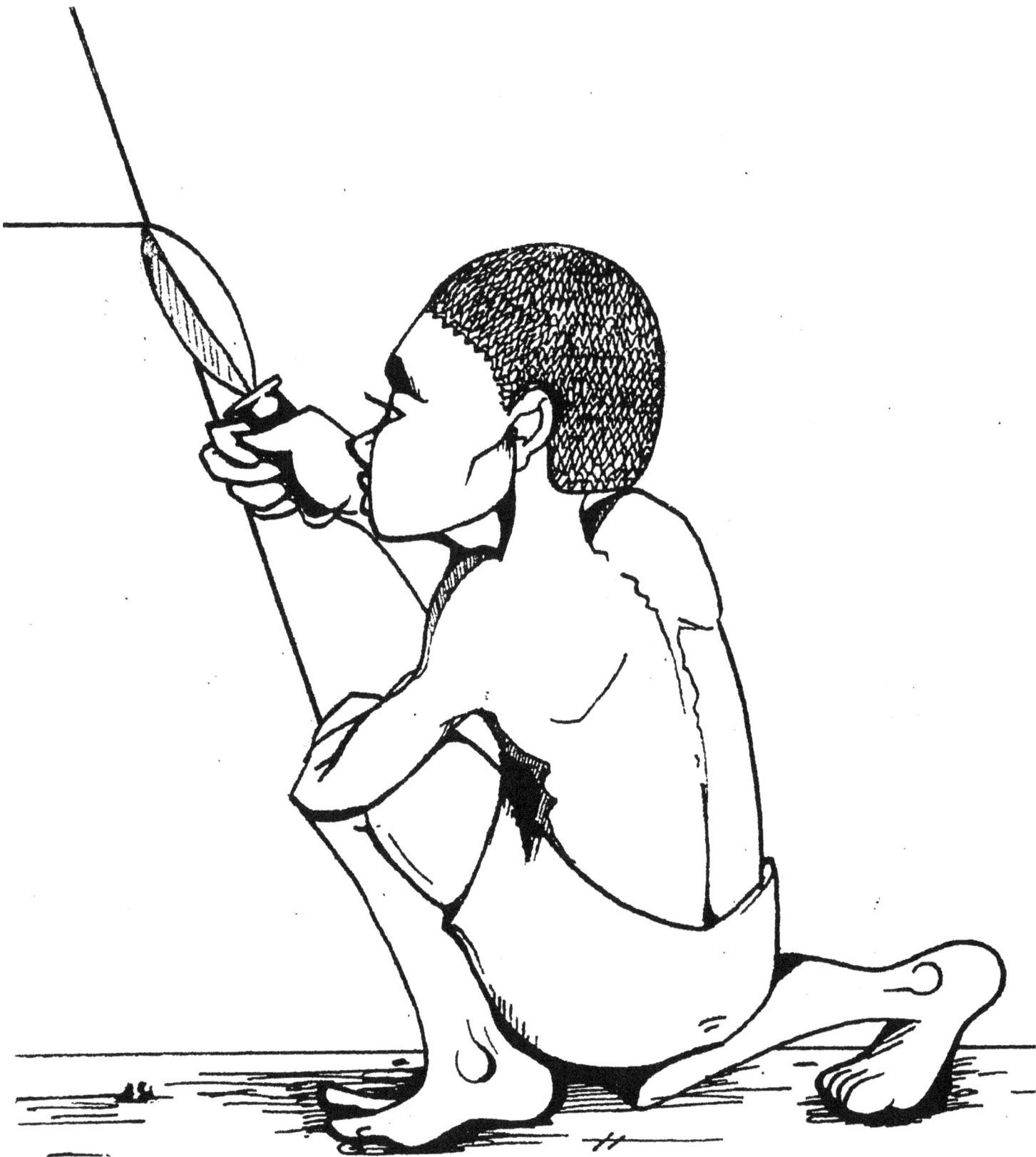

The pyramids were built without using concrete or any type of glue to hold the pyramids together. Instead, the pyramids were built by placing blocks of stone on top of each other. The African craftsmen cut the blocks so perfectly and the blocks fit so tightly on top of each other, that a knife could not fit between the blocks.

Pyramids were built using blocks that weighed from 2 tons to 70 tons. The smallest block used in building the pyramids equaled the weight of 2 cars.

Egypt

★ Memphis

Pharaoh

United States

★ Washington, D.C.

President

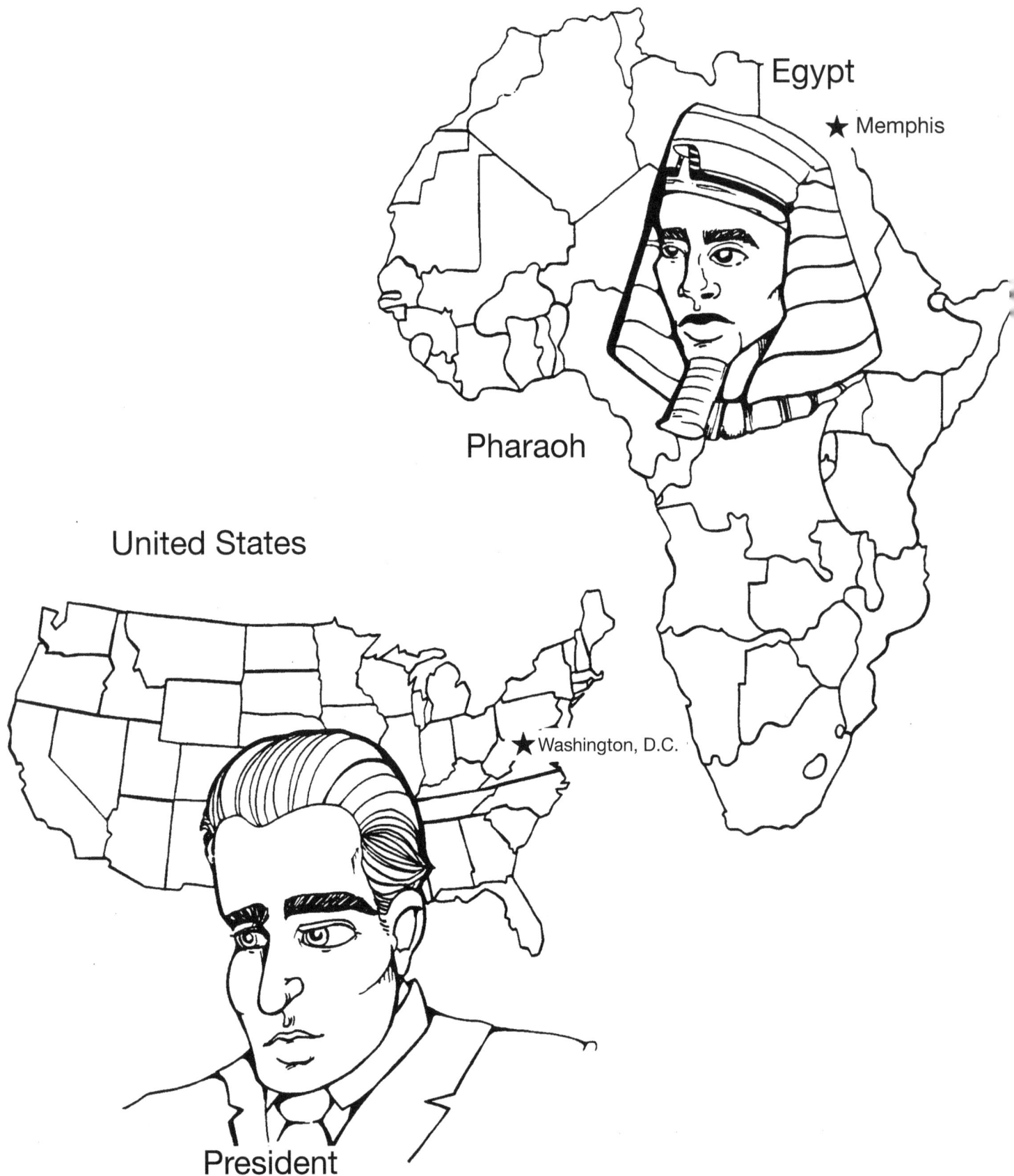

Menes created a city called Memphis to serve as the capital city for Egypt.
Memphis was the capital of Egypt like Washington, D.C. is the capital of the
United States.

Africans were experts at the craft of pottery as well as painting. Even today, African pottery is considered works of genius.

Obelisk

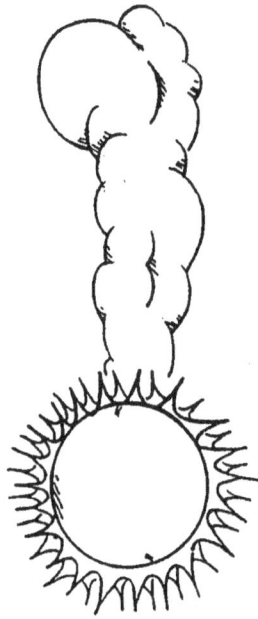

(an ancient African monument)

Washington Monument
(in modern-day Washington, DC)

African architecture was so advanced that it was the basis for some modern architecture. In fact, the Washington Monument is an exact duplicate of an African monument originally called a Tekhen (renamed later as an Obelisk).

20

Africans in Egypt created the first kind of paper and ink to write with that was small and light to carry.

African doctors had become skilled in examination, diagnosis, and treatment of over 250 illnesses. Records showed treatments of different injuries which included numerous surgical techniques.

African scientist discovered the 365 day calendar year. These scientists were the first to discover that there are 365 days in a year that can be divided into 12 months.

African people created civilization. Without African scientists, doctors, astronomers, mathematicians, and leaders, our society as we know it, would not exist. *Africans and African Americans are intelligent, beautiful people with a rich history. Everyone should know how each race has contributed to the world we know today. Take what you have learned today and share it with someone you know.*

Draw and color how life would be without ink and paper.

Africans created math. Draw and color a picture of how life would be without math.

Africans were the first to build communities. Draw and color a picture of your community (neighborhood).

Draw and color a picture of the Washington Monument and the African Monument called the Tekhen.

What tools helped build the African community? Draw and color those tools.

The first doctors were in Africa. Draw and color a trip to the doctor.

Africans built the pyramids. Draw and color a pyramid.

African scientist discovered that it takes 24 hours to have day and night. Draw and color what you do in the day and what you do at night.

Africans were the first people to farm. Draw and color some animals you might find on a farm today.

Where is Africa? Draw and color the continent of Africa.

THE BEGINNING OF CIVILIZATION
BIBLIOGRAPHY

Diop, Cheikh, <u>The African Origin of Civilization Myth or Reality</u>, Chicago, Illinois, Lawrence Hill Books, 1974.

James, George, <u>Stolen Legacy</u>, Trenton, NJ, African World Press, 1954.

Tarharka, Keita, <u>Black Manhood</u>, Washington, D.C., University Press of America, 1979.

"The Grandeur That Was Nubia," <u>The Washington Post</u>, May 10, 1995, p. H1.

"Early African Bone Tools Found," <u>The Washington Post</u>, April 28, 1995, p. A1.

Murray, Margaret, <u>The Splendor That Was Egypt</u>, New York, Philosophical Library, 1957.

www.ingramcontent.com/pod-product-compliance
Lightning Source LLC
Chambersburg PA
CBHW081243020426
42331CB00013B/3283